The Very Hungry Duck

Bernice Seward

Text © 2014 by Bernice Seward.
Illustrations © 2015 by Bernice Seward.
All rights reserved. No part of this book may be reproduced or used in any manner whatsoever without the express written permission of the publisher except for the use of brief quotations in a book review. For requests, write to Bernice Seward at PO Box 1069, Lewiston, ID 83501 or online at www.berniceseward.com

Text printed in **Quicksand** font
Duck's "tummy rumbles" printed in Engine font

ISBN: 978-0-9862879-0-9 (paperback)
ISBN: 978-0-9862879-2-3 (hardcover)

Second Edition
20 19 18 17 16 15 / 10 9 8 7 6 5 4 3

I am hungry, hungry, hungry,

and when I look, I see

a bowl upon the table

with an **apple** just for me.

Oh, no! Here comes Bunny!

Bunny eats the **apple**,
quick as quick can be.

When Bunny eats the **apple**, she leaves no bites for me!

I am hungry, hungry, hungry,
and when I look, I see

a bowl upon the table

with a **pear** just for me.

Oh, no! Here comes Puppy!

Puppy eats the **pear,**
quick as quick can be.

When Puppy eats the **pear,**
he leaves no bites for me!

I am hungry, hungry, hungry,
and when I look, I see

a bowl upon the table
with an **orange** just for me.

Oh, no, no, **no!**
Here comes **Kitty!**

Kitty eats the **orange,** quick as quick can be.

When Kitty eats the **orange,**
she leaves no bites for me!

I'm
STILL
hungry,
hungry,
hungry!

BUT . . .
when I look, I see

a bowl upon the table

with some **berries** . . . *just for me?*

I leap in with the **berries,**
quick as quick can be!

When I eat the **berries,**

www.ingramcontent.com/pod-product-compliance
Lightning Source LLC
Chambersburg PA
CBHW040731020526
44112CB00058B/2935